CONTENTS

Some words are shown in bold, **like this**. You can find out what they mean by looking in the glossary.

A pirate's job

Pirates sailed the oceans stealing from other ships. For many pirates, it was the only job they knew. Like other workers, pirates needed the right tools for the job. This included ropes, material for sails, and food and water.

Fact

Stories about pirates burying treasure on islands are probably not true. They mainly stopped at islands for fresh water and supplies.

PIRATES!

GET INTO PIRATE GEAR

Liam O'Donnell

Raintree is an imprint of Capstone Global Library Limited, a company incorporated in England and Wales having its registered office at 264 Banbury Road, Oxford OX2 7DY – Registered company number: 6695582

www.raintree.co.uk
myorders@raintree.co.uk

Edited by Bradley Cole
Designed by Kayla Dohmen
Picture research by Wanda Winch
Production by Katy LaVigne
Originated by Capstone Global Library Ltd
Printed and bound in India

ISBN 978 1 4747 4544 4 (hardback)
22 21 20 19 18 17
10 9 8 7 6 5 4 3 2 1

ISBN 978-1-4747-4548-2 (paperback)
23 22 21 20 19 18
10 9 8 7 6 5 4 3 2 1

British Library Cataloguing in Publication Data
A full catalogue record for this book is available from the British Library.

Acknowledgements
We would like to thank the following for permission to reproduce photographs: Bridgeman Images: © Look and Learn/Private Collection/Graham Coton, 25, © Look and Learn/Private Collection/Nadir Quinto, 29, © Look and Learn/Private Collection/Ron Embleton, 19, Peter Newark Historical Pictures/Private Collection/ English School, 17, Private Collection/Frederick Judd Waugh, 23, Valerie Jackson Harris Collection/© Look and Learn/Private Collection/English School, 7; iStockphoto: Kuril_solomov, cover (right); North Wind Picture Archives, 27; Shutterstock: Andrey_Kuzmin, 2–3 background, angelo gilardelli, 13, Antony McAulay, 16, Chrislofotos, 21, ilolab, vintage paper texture, Ivan Smuk, cover (flintlock pistol), Kostyantyn Ivanyshen, 5, Molodec, maps, Nik Merkulov, grunge background, pingebat, pirate icons, pjmorley, 9, Triff, cover (middle, maps bottom), nautical background, 15, tsuneomp, 11, TyBy, cover (banner).

Every effort has been made to contact copyright holders of material reproduced in this book. Any omissions will be rectified in subsequent printings if notice is given to the publisher.

Navy sailors

Many pirates had been sailors in the **navy**. The navy taught them how to find their way using only the sun and the stars as guides. Many sailors left the navy because of low wages or cruel captains.

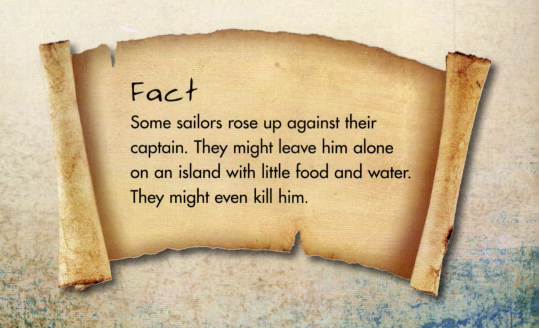

Fact

Some sailors rose up against their captain. They might leave him alone on an island with little food and water. They might even kill him.

Finding tools

Ropes, sails and pistols were all important gear for any ship. But pirates could not buy new gear at the nearest **harbour**. They risked being thrown in prison if they were caught. Instead, pirates attacked other ships and stole the things they needed.

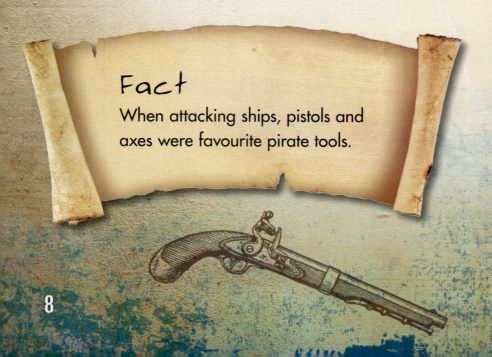

Fact

When attacking ships, pistols and axes were favourite pirate tools.

Types of gear

Sails were like engines for a pirate ship. They caught the wind and helped push the ship through the water. Each type of sail was named for its place on the ship.

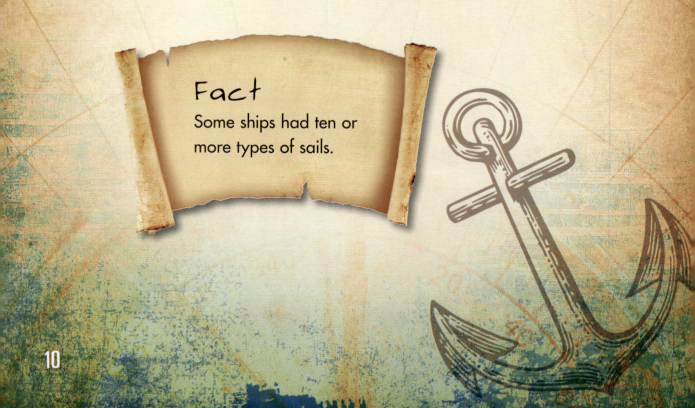

Fact
Some ships had ten or more types of sails.

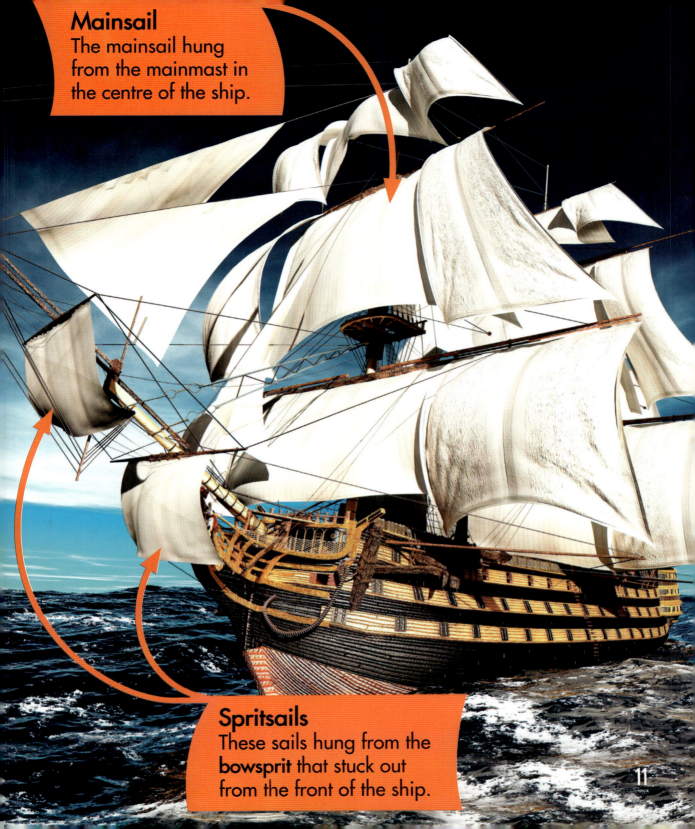

Mainsail
The mainsail hung
from the mainmast in
the centre of the ship.

Spritsails
These sails hung from the
bowsprit that stuck out
from the front of the ship.

11

Pirates had to change the sails to keep the ship moving quickly and safely. They used ropes and **pulleys** to raise and lower the sails.

Pirates used ropes called **rigging** to help them control the sails. They also had to know how to tie many types of knots.

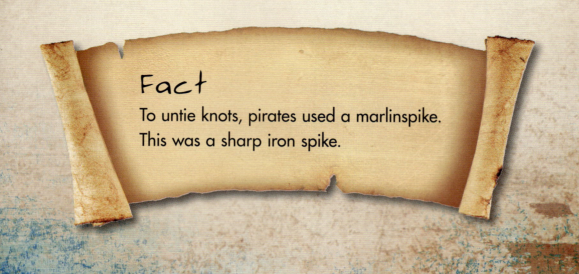

Fact

To untie knots, pirates used a marlinspike. This was a sharp iron spike.

Pirates used ocean charts. These showed where dangerous rocks, **shallow** water or safe **harbours** could be found. Sailors used **compasses** to see what direction to sail in. Sailors also used a small **telescope** called a spyglass to spot land.

Fact

Sailors used an instrument called an astrolabe to measure the position of the sun or stars. This helped them to work out their **location**.

Capturing a ship

Pirate flags struck fear into the hearts of other sailors. They were usually red or black. Pirates painted skeletons, daggers and other scary pictures onto the flags. They hoped that when ship captains saw a pirate flag, they would **surrender** without a fight.

Fact

Pirate flags were called Jolly Rogers. Early pirate flags were red. The French called them *jolie rouge*, which means "pretty red".

If the other ship didn't **surrender**, pirates would try to scare it even more. They would fire cannons or throw stink bombs onto the **deck** of the other ship. These clay jars were filled with nasty-smelling, burning **sulphur** and rotten fish guts.

Fact
Some pirate ships had their own band. They would play loud, scary music during an attack.

When the ships were close enough, the pirates used grappling hooks to move alongside the other ship. The sharp spikes of these hooks dug into the wooden **deck** of a ship. The pirates then pulled on ropes tied to the hooks to bring the two ships close together.

Fact

Grappling hooks were fired from a special cannon.

Battle

When pirates boarded another ship, its crew often **surrendered**. But sometimes they would fight a bloody battle. Short swords called cutlasses were deadly in a crowded fight. Many pirates also carried short knives called daggers. They were designed for stabbing enemies in hand-to-hand fights.

Fact

The pirates hoped that any stink bombs they had thrown would make the other ship's crew too sick to fight.

Pirates also fought with guns. The flintlock pistol was a favourite pirate weapon. It was easy to aim and small enough to carry in one hand. But the gun held only one shot. So some pirates carried several loaded pistols into battle.

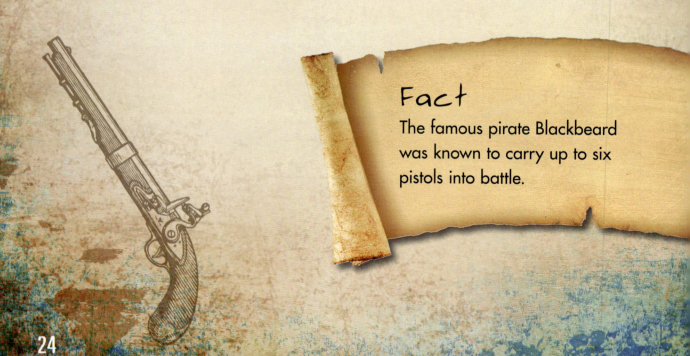

Fact

The famous pirate Blackbeard was known to carry up to six pistols into battle.

If the pirates won the battle, they would then decide what to take from the ship. This could include treasure, ship gear and supplies. They might also ask if any of the sailors wished to join them!

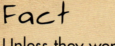

Fact

Unless they were desperate for supplies, pirates only fought battles they could easily win. If a ship looked well-armed, they left it alone.

A pirate's tools

Pirates used their gear to fight, steal treasure and sail across the ocean. Without the right tools, pirates would not have become the terror of the seas.

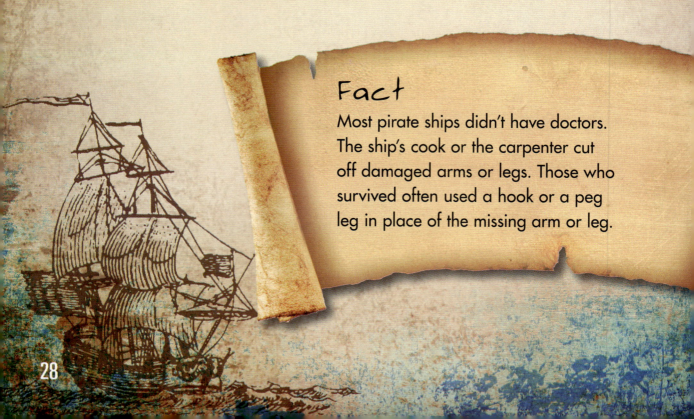

Fact

Most pirate ships didn't have doctors. The ship's cook or the carpenter cut off damaged arms or legs. Those who survived often used a hook or a peg leg in place of the missing arm or leg.

GLOSSARY

armed carrying weapons

bowsprit long pole sticking out from the front of a ship. Ropes that support the mast are attached to the bowsprit.

carpenter someone who works with wood

compass instrument used for finding direction

crew group of people who work on a ship

deck upper floor of a ship

harbour place where ships load and unload passengers and goods

location the exact place where someone or something is

mainmast tall post in the centre of a ship to which the main sails are attached

navy part of the armed services of a country that fights at sea, not on land

pulley grooved wheel that is moved by a rope. It can be used to move heavy things.

rigging ropes on a ship that support and control the sails

shallow area where water is not very deep

sulphur chemical that burns easily and is very smelly

surrender give in, admit defeat

telescope instrument that makes faraway objects seem larger and closer

FIND OUT MORE

Books

Pirate Diary (Diary Histories), Richard Platt (Walker Books, 2014)

Pirate's Handbook, Sam Taplin (Usborne, 2014)

Pirates (Horrible Histories), Terry Deary (Scholastic, 2015)

Websites

www.dkfindout.com/uk/history/pirates
Want to know about pirates? This website will tell you all you need
to know.

www.rmg.co.uk/discover/explore/life-and-times-pirate
Learn more about the lives of pirates on this website.

Places to visit

National Maritime Museum, Cornwall
Discovery Quay, Falmouth TR11 3QY
Learn all about the lives of people who have worked closely with
the sea over the centuries at the National Maritime Museum.

INDEX